Original title:
The Cosmic Quest for Purpose

Copyright © 2025 Creative Arts Management OÜ
All rights reserved.

Author: Dexter Sullivan
ISBN HARDBACK: 978-1-80566-230-3
ISBN PAPERBACK: 978-1-80566-525-0

Illuminating the Dark Matter Within

In a universe so vast and wide,
I ponder my snacks while on this ride.
A comet flies, I wave hello,
Is there room for moon cheese? I don't know!

Asteroids dance in a cosmic waltz,
But my only question: where are my socks?
Space cows moo in zero-G bliss,
While I squeeze through a galactic abyss!

Starships zoom past with reckless glee,
But I trip on stardust, oh, woe is me!
Cosmic rays give hair a wild look,
I'm the astronaut who forgot his book!

Planets spinning like a game of spin,
I wonder if life on Mars has been in.
Yet here I float with my snack attack,
Deciding if I'll ever find my way back!

Souls Adrift on Galactic Currents

In a spaceship made of cheese,
We float through stardust with ease.
As aliens wave from afar,
We forgot where we parked our car.

Finding purpose in a star fry,
We dance while we aimlessly fly.
With planets as our disco balls,
We're lost but still having ball!

Galactic Seekers in the Night

With telescopes glued to our heads,
We search for answers in our beds.
What's the meaning of a quark?
Can it bring us joy after dark?

We tried to ask a passing comet,
But it zoomed past, like "who would want it?"
So we settled for a shooting star,
And laughed, saying, "We've come so far!"

Cosmic Rhythms of the Soul

The universe has a funky beat,
As we groove with our space-age feet.
Dancing with planets round and round,
In zero gravity, we are unbound.

We shared an Uber ride with Mars,
His jokes were out of this world, like stars.
Though Venus stole the show with flair,
We figured purpose is in the air!

Queries Between Celestial Bodies

We ponder life with a moonlit gleam,
As Saturn's rings spin like a dream.
"Where are we headed?" we boldly shout,
Then trip on a meteor, dancing about!

Jupiter chuckles, saying, "Relax,
Purpose is just for cosmic hacks."
So we toss a comet, giggling loud,
And float on sunbeams, feeling proud!

The Void and the Vivid

In the dark, I lost my keys,
Floating past some space-time cheese.
Stars blinked at me with a grin,
"You'll find them, just look within!"

Galaxies dance, they play and twirl,
I tripped on stardust, gave a whirl.
Planets giggled, made some noise,
"Finding purpose? Just enjoy!"

Celestial Threads of Existence

Here I sit on a comet's tail,
Trying to write a cosmic tale.
My pen ran out, the ink's gone dry,
What's a universe without a try?

Saturn spins in a hula-hoop,
While I search for my cosmic group.
Einstein's theories float on air,
But my sandwich? Gone, nowhere!

Chasing Light Beyond Limits

I chased a photon, it was quite fast,
Fell in a black hole, but what a blast!
Starships zoom with a silly beep,
Light years away, I need more sleep!

Jupiter threw a dance-off with friends,
I showed my moves, made amends.
Cosmic chuckles filled the void,
Existence? Just a space-time toy!

Astral Reflections of the Self

In cosmic mirrors, reflections play,
I waved to myself, 'Hey, what a day!'
Laughter echoed through the dark,
Even black holes can spark a lark!

Pluto grinned, said, "You look great!"
As I pondered the meaning of fate.
Stars held hands, twirled in glee,
"Maybe it's just you and me!"

Stardust and Silent Yearnings

In the vast expanse, we twirl and spin,
Hoping to find where the fun begins.
Stars laugh as they dance with glee,
Whispering secrets, just you and me.

Galaxies giggle, play hide and seek,
With comets and asteroids, all very cheek.
Mysteries float on a cosmic breeze,
Tickling our minds like a playful tease.

Echoes of Infinity

Time stretches like a rubber band,
Where did I put my cosmic plan?
Planets are spinning in dizzying whirl,
While space dust gathers, giving it a twirl.

Black holes grin as they swallow suns,
Making galactic bets, oh what fun!
Whispers of starlight, they echo loud,
In the library of stars, nothing's quite allowed.

Celestial Dreamers

In pajamas of stardust, we dream at night,
Counting moons instead of sheep in flight.
Meteor showers make a wish list swell,
Will the universe respond? Oh, do tell!

Aliens chuckle at our earthly games,
Curious beings, with unpronounceable names.
Jumping through portals, we laugh and bounce,
Searching for purpose with every ounce.

Within the Vastness of Being

Floating 'round planets with a donut in hand,
Who knew the cosmos was perfectly planned?
Asteroids hula-hoop without a care,
While Nebulas giggle and twirl in the air.

Life's like a box of cosmic balloons,
Filled with dreams and whimsical tunes.
Finding our path among shining spheres,
With laughter echoing through all the years.

Celestial Choreography of the Heart

In a galaxy far, far away,
Cupid lost his chart today.
He shot for love but hit a cat,
Now they dance, imagine that!

Planets swirl with heart-shaped trails,
Asteroids sing, and none it fails.
Stars throw confetti, what a sight,
As aliens cheer in sheer delight!

Beyond Borders of Existence

Time travelers meet at a café,
Arguing who should pay today.
"I'm from 3020, can't you see?"
"Well, I changed history—what's your fee?"

Wormholes twist like pretzel dough,
Warp-speed jokes? They steal the show!
Dimensions bound by quirky laws,
Clapping at life's cosmic flaws!

Stories Written in Starlight

Constellations gossip in the night,
Trading tales of mythic fright.
A bear trips over a galactic pie,
While a frog hops by, oh my, oh my!

Each twinkle tells a joke on high,
A comet laughs, then zooms on by.
So grab a friend, and let's partake,
In laughter echoed through the wake!

Radiance of the Infinite

Stars wear shades to glance at Earth,
Dodging drama since their birth.
A sunbeam trips on cosmic lace,
While moons compete in a glowing race!

Galaxies swirl like carnival rides,
With quirky beings as their guides.
If laughter is light, then shine it bright,
For joy is out there, a dazzling sight!

Starlit Roads of Reflection

On a starry path, I trip and stumble,
Searching for answers, my feet start to fumble.
A comet laughs as I dance with glee,
"Purpose? Just take a leap, you'll see!"

With aliens giggling while sipping on tea,
They ask me questions, like, "Who's your VIP?"
I grin and reply, "It's the pizza guy,"
As meteors fall, I just can't deny!

Looking for meaning in asteroids flung,
I find it in laughter, that sweet, joyful song.
Stars wink at me, with cosmic delight,
It seems the answer? Just enjoy the night!

So on this starlit road, with friends by my side,
We create a purpose, in joy we confide.
Who needs a map when you have a full heart?
In this galaxy of giggles, that's just the start!

Navigating the Celestial Labyrinth

In a maze of stars, I wander confused,
Every twist and turn feels a bit abused.
A black hole whispers, "You missed the way!"
I chuckle back, "Guess I'll stay here and play!"

A space skip-hop, I jump through the haze,
Finding lost socks in interstellar bays.
A Martian with snacks, says, "Join the fun!"
I ponder if purpose is just a sweet bun.

Galactic GPS says, "Recalculating!"
But here in the stars, I'm joyfully waiting.
With quirky aliens offering hugs so wide,
I find my direction, with laughter as guide!

So if you're lost in this cosmic game,
Remember, it's fun that truly brings fame.
Exploration is grand, but joy is the key,
In this labyrinth of light, let's just be free!

Echoes of Distant Galaxies

The stars sing stories, and I pause to hear,
Echoes of laughter float far and near.
A pulsar's pulse makes my heart skip a beat,
Is that the sound of joy, or just my two left feet?

The universe giggles, at jokes alien-made,
While they toast to tequila, in cosmic parade.
With cosmic confetti, they dance through the void,\nFinding that silliness can't be destroyed.

Black holes may pull, but I'm not in a rush,
For in space there's humor, in every big hush.
I step on a star, trip over a quark,
And find that my purpose is really quite stark!

So listen for echoes, they're funny for sure,
In the great vast beyond, laughter is pure.
With each cosmic quip, we discover with cheer,
Our journey unfolds, with joy as our steer!

Through Cosmic Mirrors We Seek

In mirrors of stars, reflections collide,
I see my mischievous self, what a ride!
With space bendy straws, I sip on the light,
Each bubble a moment, oh what a sight!

Warped by the laughter, I float through the skies,
While meteors juggle, what a sweet surprise!
"Purpose is tricky!" a nebula agrees,
"But joy is the answer, now pass me the cheese!"

Galaxies shimmer, like disco-ball dreams,
Finding my path in a world of moonbeams.
I swing on a comet, in laughter I trust,
In this cosmic maze, it's the fun that's a must!

So through these reflections, I twist and I twirl,
With cosmos as my stage, I begin to unfurl.
In the mirrors of joy, our purpose we find,
In the dance of the stars, we're all intertwined!

Threads of Fate in the Cosmos

In a galaxy not far away,
A cat found a stars' buffet.
She licked a comet with glee,
Said, 'This is the life for me!'

Aliens danced in odd pairs,
Wearing shirts of solar flares.
They giggled and tickled the sun,
'Our party's just begun!'

A spaceship full of socks,
Crashed on Planet of the Rocks.
They argued about which was best,
Blue polka dots beat red, no jest!

So if you seek your fate's own cheer,
Look for laughter, let it steer.
The cosmos smiles, it's not a bore,
Just keep looking, there's always more!

Echoes of the Infinite Journey

Once a wanderer lost at sea,
He asked stars, 'What's wrong with me?'
They blinked and giggled in delight,
Said, 'You forgot to wear your light!'

He built a boat from meteor dust,
Promised the moon he'd be robust.
Yet every wave told him a joke,
As he drifted in cosmic smoke.

He pirouetted past a quasar,
Danced like a very clumsy star.
With each swirl he snorted a laugh,
Swore he was part of the galactic staff!

So on this journey, friends, just know,
The path is wild, let laughter flow.
In echoes of time and places vast,
It's the fun, not the goal, that's meant to last!

Stardust Dreams and Celestial Schemes

In a nebula swirling in pink,
A squirrel sipped coffee and blinked.
He pondered the mysteries of space,
While plotting an interstellar race.

With asteroids shaped like cheese wheels,
He served them to his lost dog Reels.
'Galactic pizza is all the rage!'
They munched away, joy on the stage.

A robot appeared with a hat,
Said, 'My calculations, where are they at?'
But the squirrel just laughed till he bled,
'You're not getting cheese, just go ahead!'

So dream big with twinkling schemes,
Dance with stars, ignite your dreams.
In this universe, full of crazed spins,
Embrace the silly where laughter begins!

Whispers of the Infinite

Countless whispers float on air,
Telling tales of time and flair.
A wise old comet passed by me,
Said, 'Life's a joke, just wait and see!'

A star went shopping for a new hat,
Complained that it was far too flat.
A wisecrack winked from Saturn's rings,
'Wear it with pride, oh cosmic king!'

Planets chuckled, spinning tight,
Moons rolling with pure delight.
Said, 'Who needs a map or a coach?
Just ride the waves like a cosmic roach!'

So when you ponder your grand design,
Remember to dance, sip some wine.
In whispers of the vast unknown,
Find the laughter that's your own!

Navigating the Universe Within

In the depths of my mind, I took a ride,
Searching for answers where the thoughts reside.
Found a sock in a nebula full of dreams,
Slipped on a comet, or so it seems.

I asked my brain for a map, oh dear,
It led me to pizza, with extra cheese near.
The stars kept chuckling, bright in their glow,
While I pondered if I should go fast or slow.

With every thought, a new galaxy spun,
Was it enlightenment or just having fun?
I rode on a quasar and danced on a beam,
In the end, all I found was a laugh and a dream.

Whispers of the Infinite

The whispers of space tickle my ear,
As I float through the void, sipping on beer.
Celestial giggles echo so bright,
Perhaps Pluto's the punchline—I'll laugh all night.

A shooting star winked as it zipped right by,
I waved it a cheer, oh my, oh my!
The Milky Way's chuckles shake up the dark,
While I scribble poems on a lunar park.

Caught a glimpse of time, what a pesky thing,
It wrapped me in jokes, made my heart sing.
Infinity's pranks keep me hopping around,
In this cosmic circus, joy can be found.

The Dance of Celestial Souls

Stars are the dancers in the sky's grand ball,
Waltzing on wishes, they rise and they fall.
Meteor showers sprinkle the floor with delight,
As planets spin laughter into the night.

I tripped over Venus and slipped on her shine,
But laughed it off—cosmic humor's divine!
Orion rolled over to share a big grin,
Said, 'Join the dance! Where do I begin?'

Galaxies shimmy with a twinkling glee,
While black holes chuckle—'It's a mystery!'
Each cosmic twirl's a quirky surprise,
In this zany ballet, joy never dies.

Starlit Paths of Discovery

With starlit paths beneath my feet,
I wander through dreams, oh so sweet.
A nebula giggled, 'You're lost, my friend,'
I shrugged and replied, 'Does it matter in the end?'

Through asteroid fields, I do a jig,
Where each giant rock wears a dance-wear big.
I found a planet doing the cha-cha slide,
And spun to its rhythm with cosmic pride.

Exploring these realms, what a whimsical sight,
My compass spins wildly, but that feels just right.
Each step is a punchline, a joke under stars,
In this grand cosmic quest, we're all just bizarre.

Beyond the Grasp of Time

To catch a clock, I chase my shoes,
But time just laughs, it plays its ruse.
I trip on seconds, fall in a blur,
As minutes giggle, their jokes a stir.

I asked a sundial for advice,
It told me slow down, which was quite nice.
But shadows wink, and off they sprint,
While I just ponder: What's the hint?

I wore a watch made of bubblegum,
It melted away, but oh, what fun!
In this great race of tick and tock,
I'll dance with space, my feet will rock.

So here I am, a jester in time,
With laughter echoing in cosmic rhyme.
As I chase the stars, they wink at me,
Saying, "Just enjoy, let yourself be free!"

Nebulae of Inspiration

I looked up high, saw clouds of fluff,
They whispered dreams, but lacked the stuff.
A comet sneezed, and stars erupted,
In this bright mess, I felt interrupted.

A quasar laughed—what a disco ball!
It spun so fast, I began to fall.
With every twinkle, a funny thought,
Life's a joke, and we're all caught!

Asteroids danced, they called me names,
"Clumsy human, we play silly games!"
Yet in this chaos, I found my muse,
From cosmic folly, I'd never snooze.

So here I stand, on this wild ride,
With bits of stardust, I'm filled with pride.
The universe smiled, it said, "Just light up,
And let your laughter be the way to sup!"

Renegades of the Cosmic Tide

A starship crew with mismatched dreams,
Sailing through space on coffee streams.
With every leap, a clumsy twirl,
Around black holes, we spin and whirl.

Captain said, "Don't eat that green goo,"
It opened a wormhole, who knew?
We laughed so hard, we flew off course,
Chasing a comet, it felt like a horse!

The alien gave us jellybeans,
Said "They're magic, trade your routines!"
We danced in zero-gravity gloom,
As colors changed and filled the room.

So here we are, lost, but full of cheer,
Making the galaxies our own frontier.
With giggles echoing through the void,
A cosmic riot with laughter employed!

Beneath the Stars of Significance

Beneath the sky, I sipped my tea,
Spilled it all over, oh, woe is me!
The constellations giggled bright,
As I tried to find wisdom in their light.

I asked Orion for a fun quest,
He just winked and said, "No rest!"
But shooting stars were breaking loose,
Chasing mishaps, they let me loose!

The moon made jokes, a wise old chap,
Told me, "Life's a big cosmic flap!"
So I grinned wide at this lunatic sage,
Embracing the chaos, my own cosmic stage.

Under this blanket of stellar threads,
I learned to laugh instead of dread.
For when you dance with the universe's tune,
Every misstep can lead to a boon!

Dancing with Celestial Starlight

In a galaxy far, far away,
Stars wear shoes made of bright sunray.
They twirl and spin in a cosmic ball,
While planets giggle, having a ball.

Asteroids throw confetti at will,
Black holes joke, 'We're just a drill!'
Comets dash like kids on a spree,
Shooting stars shout, 'Look at me!'

Wormholes play hide and seek with time,
While stardust sprinkles, oh so prime.
Constellations keep making new trends,
As moonbeams giggle, freedom transcends.

So let's laugh under this cosmic night,
For joy is the universe's delight.
Dance with the starlight, feel the cheer,
In the cosmic party, everyone's near!

Journeys Beyond the Event Horizon

A spaceship zoomed past the chaos grand,
Captain grinned, 'We've got a wild plan!'
Through twisting beams and quantum quirks,
It's a ride where nothing really works!

Aliens waved with a goofy face,
'Welcome aboard to the time-travel race!'
With spaghetti strings and rubber ducks,
We laughed through space, all kinds of lucks.

Gravity? Just a suggestion, I swear,
We toss planets like they're light as air.
Falling through loops, who needs a bed?
In zero G, we just laugh instead.

So if you see us through the galactic maze,
Serving snacks for interstellar gaze.
Join our fun, don't be a bore,
In the universe, there's always more!

Spheres of Wonder and Cosmic Whimsy

Orbs of light, spinning round with glee,
Whirling so fast, can't catch me!
Glittering dust in a vibrant swirl,
Spheres of wonder, let's give it a twirl.

Asteroids popping like fizzy drinks,
Made of chocolate? Who even thinks!
The moons pull pranks, they launch rock pies,
While Saturn giggles, bright ringed goodbyes.

Nebulas frolic like kids at play,
Blowing bubbles that float away.
'Catch me if you can!' the stars they shout,
As comets streak past, racing about.

In this cosmic circus, no one feels blue,
With laughter echoing from me to you.
So join the fun, let your spirit roam,
In the universe, we find our home!

Nirvana in the Nebula

In soft clouds of gas, we find our way,
Chasing rainbows in the Milky Way.
Stars play sit-and-seek with our dreams,
While goofy meteors burst out in beams.

Floating through colors, we giggle and drift,
Finding the cosmos is quite the gift.
With whirls of laughter, we paint the skies,
Shooting for joy, oh how time flies!

Black holes whisper secrets of the night,
"Come closer, dear friend, it's a beautiful sight!"
But don't get sucked in, just take a peek,
A fun cosmic riddle, unique and mystique.

So let's sail through the nebula's glow,
With giggles and whimsy, let good vibes flow.
For in this vast expanse, we'll never be lost,
In the laughter of stars, we celebrate most!

A Journey Through the Celestial Veil

I once met a star with a funky hat,
It said, "Life's a dance, but don't forget your cat!"
We twirled through the ether with some cosmic flair,
While comets played music, floating through the air.

Planets queued up for their selfie glow,
"Say cheese!" shouted Mars, stealing the show.
Dancing in space, no gravity in sight,
Who knew the Milky Way could have such a bite?

Nebulas whispered their colorful tunes,
As we giggled with moons beneath sparkling dunes.
"What's the meaning?" I pondered, all lost in the fun,
"Maybe it's pizza under the bright cosmic sun!"

With laughter and light, we soared past the veil,
Chasing the stars on a whimsical trail.
Slipping on stardust in a galactic glide,
Turns out, this journey is one wild ride!

Radiance Among Shadows

In a galaxy far, where shadows do prance,
We found a bright orb, hosting a dance.
"Join us!" it beckoned, glimmering bright,
"We waltz with our dark side every moonlight!"

Stars were sip-sipping, through cosmic brew,
While asteroids honked and a meteor flew.
"Is this the meaning?" we questioned with glee,
"Maybe it's brunch under Jupiter's sea!"

A black hole whispered secrets, or was that a joke?
As planets all chuckled, their rings went up in smoke.
"Your purpose is clear, just giggle and spin,
Even in shadows, let the laughter begin!"

So, we twirled and we swayed, no worries in place,
Finding joy in the chaos, a merry embrace.
In radiance found among shadows so dear,
We danced our way through, with laughter and cheer!

Celestial Tornadoes of Meaning

In the middle of space, a twister did swirl,
With stardust confetti, it began to unfurl.
"Hold on tight!" shouted Venus, with a wink,
As we whirled and we laughed, dancing on the brink.

Asteroids shouted, "What's the deal?"
While Saturn made snacks, spinning meals with zeal.
"Is this the purpose?" a quasar inquired,
"Or just cosmic chaos, hilariously plired?"

Through the tornado of thoughts, we spun with delight,
Dodging black holes that bumbled in fright.
"Grab the spaghetti!" yelled a star with a grin,
"Essence of meaning? Let the fun begin!"

When the storm settled down, with giggles so bright,
We realized our journey turned chaos to light.
With laughter as fuel, as we spun in the tides,
The meaning was clear—it's the joy that abides!

Seekers of the Stellar Horizon

We set off on rockets shaped like a fish,
With dreams of the cosmos and a cosmic dish.
"Are we seekers?" I asked, while flying through space,
"Or just hungry travelers, lost in the race?"

Planets were roasting marshmallows on fire,
While aliens chanted their favorite choir.
"Purpose!" they shouted, tossing pies from above,
"Maybe purpose is pizza, or something we love!"

So off we went, with our goofy parade,
Singing with comets, enjoying the shade.
The stellar horizon teased with its gleam,
"Is this all a joke?" I began to dream.

And as we glided through nebulae vast,
We learned every moment is meant to hold fast.
With giggles and joy, we crafted a tune,
As seekers of laughter beneath a bright moon!

The Silent Symphony of the Stars

In the night, the stars all gleam,
A cosmic dance, a silly dream.
They twinkle down with a wink and grin,
'Who forgot the music? Let's begin!'

A comet zooms with style and flair,
Dodging asteroids like it just don't care.
The Milky Way throws a wild party,
But gravity's got a plan that's hearty.

Black holes laugh, pulling in the light,
'We're the life of this interstellar night!'
While planets spin in goofy circles,
One says, 'I'm baked—call me a urkel!'

So here we float in this grand jest,
Searching for meaning, we're quite the pest.
With every star, a giggle or two,
Who needs a map when the fun's in view?

Reflections in the Celestial Sea

Splashing stardust in the cosmic tide,
Mermaids giggle as they joyfully ride.
The little fish say, 'Is that a UFO?'
One flicks its fins, says, 'Watch me go!'

Waves of light dance across the sky,
'Is that a crab?' a shooting star asks shy.
With constellations weaving their plot,
Each shimmering hint asks, 'What have we forgot?'

Swirling planets make a big ol' splash,
While meteors zoom like a tasty hash.
The universe beckons like a big blue sea,
'Jump in, my friend, don't think it's just me!'

Reflections ripple, revealing our dreams,
Galactic giggles and whimsical beams.
Oh, the fun of floating here we'll seize,
In this quirky void, let's just be at ease!

Mapping the Cosmic Heart

Where do we go in this vast expanse?
The stars are winking, let's take a chance.
Plotting paths on an old pizza map,
'Who ordered this? A cosmic trap?'

Asteroids bounce like they don't have a care,
While meteors shout, 'Catch me if you dare!'
Each black hole grins with a mischievous spark,
'Don't take that route—come dance in the dark!'

Epic journeys in a broken-down ship,
Navigating love's mistaken grip.
'Is that a planet, or just a big bubble?'
'Don't land there, friend, it's all just trouble!'

So let's paint the stars with laughter so bright,
In this cosmic canvas, let's bring the light.
With every beat of the universe' heart,
We giggle and play, that's the best part!

Galaxies of Thought and Dream

In a galaxy far, far away,
Thoughts frolic like children at play.
Where dreams bounce around on inflatable beams,
And reality's lost in whimsical themes.

Ideas fly like kites in the sky,
While shooting thoughts go zipping by.
'Hey, what's that? A dream in disguise?'
'Just my imagination in a silly surprise!'

Stars giggle and shine in playful delight,
Mixing up dreams that take off in flight.
Ideas collide in a colorful swirl,
Spinning and twirling, oh what a whirl!

So join this fun, a swirling parade,
In galaxies bright where laughter is made.
With thoughts and dreams hopping to and fro,
Let's dance through the cosmos—come on, let's go!

Unraveling the Mysteries of the Milky Way

Stars wink at me from afar,
Like they know my dinner plans.
A black hole sues for damages,
Turns out it swallowed my socks.

I ask a comet for directions,
It zooms by with a gasp and laughs.
Galaxies spin in a dance,
Like they're just part of the act.

Mars is eating all my snacks,
Venus quotes Shakespeare with flair.
Jupiter's throwing a rave tonight,
While Saturn's rings catch all the hair.

So here I float, a cosmic clown,
Chasing stars in this grand parade.
Life's a joke from every angle,
And I'm just part of the charade.

Voices in the Cosmic Wind

Listen close to the whispers,
Of planets sharing gossip tips.
Mercury's always in a rush,
While Neptune takes snappy trips.

The sun tells tales of wild parties,
While moons roll their eyes in jest.
Asteroids throw popcorn at comets,
This weekend? A meteor fest!

Stars call out with hilarious puns,
Black holes sigh with cosmic dread.
Space dust scattered like confetti,
From an interstellar wedding spread.

Laughter echoes through vast space,
Each giggle drifting with the breeze.
The universe, a stand-up show,
Where time's punchlines bring me to my knees.

Journeying Through Celestial Echoes

I packed my bags for a moonlit trip,
But forgot to bring my shoes.
Floating past some asteroids,
Made me question travel news.

Saturn's rings are like a hula,
While Pluto just slows to wave.
A supernova sent me flying,
I laughed as I hit a space cave.

Aliens served up space tacos,
With a side of cosmic fries.
They claim the best sauce is moonlight,
But I just can't believe their lies.

And as I drift through starry dreams,
I ponder all that I've embraced.
In this voyage of pure nonsense,
I find my smile wrapped in space.

Asteroids of Aspiration

Asteroids rolling like bowling balls,
Chasing my dreams across the space.
I tried to outrun a shooting star,
But it just giggled and kept the pace.

Crafting wishes on not-so-bright sparks,
Turns out they're just runaway lights.
Voices echoing from below,
Ask me if I'll ever take flight.

Galaxies spinning with wild plans,
They say 'Aim high, don't hit the sun.'
But I'm just here munching stardust,
Wondering if I'll ever have fun.

So I'll dance on these rocky paths,
With dreams bigger than my space suit.
Because if space can laugh with me,
Then why not? I'm ready to scoot!

Reflections of a Starry Mind

In a galaxy where laughter soared,
I questioned if my thoughts were floored.
Is Pluto just a shy old friend?
Or do his icebergs just pretend?

Comets zoom like kids on a spree,
They dodge my wishes and flee from me.
Stars giggle as they twinkle bright,
Whispering dreams of cosmic flight.

Journeying Through Astral Realms

Floating through the Milky Way,
I lost my map, oh what a day!
Aliens offered me a ride,
They honked and laughed, a comical glide.

Asteroids danced a funky jig,
While black holes played cards—oh so big!
I asked a nebula for advice,
It hiccuped stardust, oh so nice.

Birth of Dreams in the Cosmos

In the womb of space where wishes bloom,
I tried to sweep away the gloom.
With each star born, a chuckle shared,
Who knew the universe really cared?

Planets argued over who's the best,
While satellites took a cosmic rest.
I brewed a potion of light and glee,
And danced with meteors wild and free.

Threads of Fate Across the Universe

Tangled threads weave tales unknown,
As space-time laughs at mishaps sown.
A fortune cookie from a quasar said,
'Be bold, eat snacks, and forge ahead!'

Each planet spins a yarn quite twisted,
While stardust giggles, never missed it.
The cosmos shines with a wink and nod,
In this grand play, we're all just flawed.

Orbits of Thought in a Cosmic Sea

In a galaxy far, far away,
Thoughts spin like comets in play.
Searching for answers amidst the stars,
But all we find are friendly Mars bars.

Jupiter giggles as Saturn spins,
While aliens munch on popcorn skins.
We ponder existence with glee and cheer,
Then trip on stardust with a clumsy rear.

Group chats happen on solar flares,
Where asteroids dance with nary a care.
We're stargazers lost, yet so well-fed,
As we laugh at the stars from our soft, comfy bed.

A cosmic comedy, who knew we'd embark?
With black holes that swallow the snacks left in the park.
As the universe chuckles, we take a sip,
Oh, what a ride on this galactic trip!

Epiphanies in the Ether

In the void, bubbles of thought arise,
Like fizzy drinks to open the skies.
Each spark of genius, a pop and a fizz,
Yet landing on Earth, we just stand and whizz.

Transmissions of wisdom in waves that arrive,
A cosmic email that can't quite contrive.
With subjects like 'Why do socks always stray?'
We ponder the depths, then blink—what a day!

Space whales sing tunes to the moonlight's glow,
While constellations twirl in a cosmic show.
Finding some meaning in life's funny game,
And realizing that we're all just the same.

So here's to the questions, the mixed-up replies,
As we dance with our whims and gaze at the fries.
Epiphanies bobbing like boats on the wave,
In the ether of nonsense, we chuckle and rave!

Beyond the Horizon of Understanding

There's a border where questions turn into laughs,
Like dodging a comet while checking the charts.
With every new riddle, we frolic and swing,
Under banners of curiosity—what will it bring?

Gravitational pull of dreams must be light,
As we stretch our minds through the quirky twilight.
Why do bananas always wear a grin?
And is that where all our ponderings begin?

We gallop through time, dressed in pixie dust,
With purpose akin to the quirkiest gust.
Beyond the horizon, absurdity reigns,
With laughter that taps on our cosmic brains.

So come take a ride on this zany kite,
Where meaning is juggled, but it feels just right.
In the big cosmic scheme, we're all just a part,
Of the humorous quest that's tickling the heart!

The Infinite Odyssey of Meaning

In an infinite loop of curious thoughts,
We dance with absurdity, twist with our knots.
Running in circles around the bright sun,
As we stumble on answers and giggle for fun.

Why do stars twinkle with so much delight?
Perhaps they're just warming up for a night.
In endless debates with intelligent beans,
All pondering life in our humorous dreams.

Orbits we travel, sometimes with flair,
With hiccups and giggles—who really would care?
Purpose is silly, a duck in a hat,
As we frolic through space, oh fancy that!

So off we will go on this strange, cosmic ride,
With laughter as fuel, there's nothing to hide.
In the infinite dance of what's brave and what's keen,
We'll stick to the fun, while chasing the unseen!

Parallax of the Soul

In the vast skies, I thought I'd dive,
Looking for answers, man, what a jive!
Stars waved goodbye, said, 'Not today!'
With my trusty telescope, I lost my way.

I asked a comet, 'Where's my next stop?'
It laughed out loud, 'Maybe a soda pop!'
Planets tumbled, tripping in space,
While I just floated, lost in my grace.

Galaxies giggled, twinkling so bright,
Said, 'Hey, buddy, give it a night!'
I danced with the moons in a silly swirl,
Feeling superior in my cosmic twirl.

Earth pulled me back, with its gentle tug,
"Let's grab a burger, don't be a mug!"
So here I stand, with fries in tow,
Searching for meaning in the night's glow.

Celestial Cartographers of Fate

With maps of stardust, they scribble and giggle,
Charting the cosmos, oh what a wiggle!
'Left or right, should we spin?' they query,
As meteors race, making all things merry.

'Follow the Milky Way, see where it bends!'
They argue with asteroids, making new friends.
Starships are parked in a cosmic lane,
While butterflies wonder if they'll ride the train.

Space squirrels giggle, plotting their day,
Mapping the universe in a funny way.
'Check out that black hole, should we take a peek?'
Oh, how they laugh, 'Blown away? Not this week!'

Laughter and starlight, a whimsical blend,
Discoveries await around every bend.
When curiosity reigns, it's all just a game,
And we're the players, though never the same.

The Universe Within Our Bones

In the deep of my wrist, a black hole resides,
Pulled in by the donuts, what a wild ride!
My knees creaked and moaned, like a funky tune,
I must be a planet, spinning 'round the moon.

Galaxies swirling in my wobbly spine,
Each hiccup a quasar, feeling just fine.
So I shimmy and shake, while stars shake their heads,
'He's made of stardust, and maybe some breads.'

With laughter in toasts, we drink cosmic beer,
Old atoms gossiping, oh, what a cheer!
Celestial cravings, sweet chocolate surprise,
It's hard being star stuff in this human disguise.

Gravity holds me, but I want to bounce,
Floating through life, not a care to pounce.
So let's giggle together, as our atoms collide,
In the weirdest of dances, nothing to hide.

Harmonies of the Celestial Symphony

The universe plays tunes that make no sense,
Like cats on pianos, a vast recompense.
Neutron stars hum in vibrato so deep,
While I just hum back, wondering how to leap.

Pluto joins in, with a kazoo in hand,
Blowing cosmic notes that are perfectly bland.
A symphony's chaos, each star burst a joke,
While Venus in disco shoes starts to poke.

Supernovae pop like popcorn in air,
A rhythm of laughter, no need for despair.
As comets join forces, they break into swing,
Playing round with black holes, oh what fun they bring!

So dance, twirl and laugh with the starlit brigade,
Life's a grand concert, the universe played.
In this cosmic choir, we're all just a part,
Making merry in tune with a tickled-up heart.

Seeking Significance in a Celestial Dance

In the vastness of space, I twirl and spin,
Wondering if this dance is where I begin.
Stars chuckle above as they blink and sway,
'Just enjoy the show, kid, it's a cosmic ballet!'

Comets zoom by with a wink and a wave,
They leave me a trail of stardust to save.
I ponder my fate with a grin on my face,
Did I sign up for this wild, wacky race?

Planets chatter like gossiping friends,
Sharing their secrets, it never quite ends.
I think that I'm lost in this starry expanse,
But maybe I'm meant for the quirkiest dance!

Galaxies giggle, they swirl and collide,
Laughing at me on this cosmic joyride.
Maybe my purpose is simply to laugh,
And enjoy my odd journey along the star path!

Planetary Pilgrimages and Poetic Paths

Set out on a trip to the planets afar,
My spaceship's a toaster, my guide—a guitar.
Singing to Saturn, a tune full of cheer,
While Mars rolls its eyes, 'Oh, not this again, dear!'

Neptune brings snacks, shaped like little whales,
I munch on blue cookies while I gather tales.
Jupiter joins with a dance so grand,
'Just float with the rhythm of the starry band!'

The sun plays the lute; oh, what a delight!
He warms up the crowd, igniting the night.
With cosmic confetti, we celebrate we,
Who knew finding fun was the key to be free?

As I trek through the cosmos, odd sights to unfold,
I gather the laughter, more precious than gold.
In this grand journey, I find joy anew,
And maybe that's purpose, just having a view!

The Light of Stars and Inner Fire

Stars shimmer like candles in a cosmic cake,
I blow out the wishes, oh, make no mistake.
But what if the wishes are just frosting sweet?
And joy is the spark that makes life complete?

I chase after starlight, it giggles and teases,
Through nebulous clouds, my spirit feels breezy.
A blackout cup filled with stardust divine,
I sip on the essence of all things benign!

Each planet shines brightly with tales to recount,
Mercury whispers secrets, oh dear, quite the amount!
But I'm here for the laughs and the games we can play,
While Saturn spins rings, I'm just here for the sway.

In the glittering vastness, I dance with delight,
While galaxies gather for a dance party night.
I might not find answers in ticking the time,
But the joy in this madness feels exceedingly fine!

Chaos and Harmony in Celestial Realms

In the chaos of stars, where comets collide,
I laugh at the mess, it's a wacky ride!
Galaxies swirl with a clumsy embrace,
While Pluto just frowns, 'Am I still in this race?'

Supernovas go pop like confetti on high,
And I giggle as stardust rains down from the sky.
What's purpose, you ask, when the universe spins?
I'd say it's the laughter that joy brings within!

In the harmony of silence, I stand with delight,
As the cosmos hums softly, a fabulous night.
Each black hole's a joke that the universe tells,
And I'm just the jester, who giggles and dwells.

Through chaos and calmness where starlight may beam,
I find my own rhythm, lost in a dream.
So if you're searching for meaning sublime,
Join in on the fun, it's the best way to climb!

Shadows Cast by Celestial Light

Stars are shining down on me,
But I forgot where I parked, you see.
Constellations guide my way,
Yet I stumble on my socks today.

Asteroids zoom right past my head,
Joking that I'm stuck in bed.
While comets race in cosmic ballet,
I'm just hoping it's pizza night today.

Awakening Under the Celestial Dome

Woke up today beneath the stars,
Wondering where I left my car.
Aliens gossip in the sky,
About my dreams—oh my, oh my!

Planets swirl in a celestial dance,
While I stumble in my pants.
Gravity's just a mean old friend,
Who keeps my snacks from me, I contend.

Moons of Mind and Celestial Dreams

Moons spin tales of tofu and cheese,
While I ponder if I should sneeze.
Galactic giggles fill the air,
As I contemplate my comb-over hair.

Nebulas whisper sweet lullabies,
While I search for my favorite fries.
With each light-year, I try to be wise,
But can't recall where I left my pies.

Seeking Significance in Cosmic Currents

Stars are twinkling, oh what a sight,
But I forgot to turn on the light.
Neutron stars just want to jest,
Do they know I failed that math test?

Wormholes twist in a cosmic spree,
While I can't find my other shoe, whee!
In the vastness, I fumble and trot,
Trying to find what I forgot.

Searching for Meaning Among the Stars

I looked at Jupiter, thought he was wise,
A giant with questions, not much of a prize.
His rings did laugh, like a circus of fun,
While I scratched my head, wondering what I'd won.

Venus teased Mars, in a dance up so high,
"Why chase after answers?" she winked with a sigh.
But comets just zipped by, making me blink,
As if the universe said, "Just grab a drink!"

Saturn's great storms had a ticklish jest,
"Why seek out your purpose? You're doing your best!"
My heart found a rhythm, I started to sway,
Cosmic chaos around me, I laughed all the way.

Stars winked in delight at my silly spree,
Maybe meaning is found in a dance, not decree.
With laughter my guide, I floated along,
What a whimsical journey, too funny to be wrong!

Harmonies of the Celestial Orchestra

In the galaxy's band, the moon took the lead,
With stars as the chorus, they played on indeed.
They strummed silly strings, harmonized with glee,
While asteroids danced, setting chaos free.

"Hey Sun!" crooned the stars, "You're burning so bright!
But can you play tuba? It might be a sight!"
Each planet had talents, some serious, some not,
Like Neptune's bad jokes in an interstellar spot.

Black holes chimed in with a gravitational pull,
"Join us if you dare, but don't be a fool!"
As quasars did tap dances, spinning in time,
Here on this stage, everything's just sublime.

So join in the fun, create your own tune,
Among the vast heavens, you'll feel like a loon.
With laughter and music, let's drift without care,
In this cosmic orchestra, we all have a share!

Quest for the Essence of Being

Deep in the cosmos, I fumbled for sense,
Each thought like a comet, just way too intense.
Asteroids chuckled, "What's with all the fuss?
You'd rather just float, without all that bus."

The meaning of life slipped my grasp like a fish,
I asked a wise nebula, "Hey, what's your wish?"
She puffed out her clouds and just giggled with glee,
"Be silly, enjoy, that's the essence, you see!"

A quasar piped up, "A game, let's all play!
Who can find meaning in the silliest way?"
With giggles and gags, we flew through the void,
Finding joy in the chaos, never annoyed.

Each planet a joker, shared jests as we spun,
In this cosmic charade, we all had our fun.
So if seeking for meaning has left you confused,
Chase laughter and smiles, you can't be accused!

Celestial Oracles of Destiny

Under the starlight, I sought wisdom rare,
But the oracles laughed, tossing giggles in air.
"Dear traveler, destiny's a whimsical ride,
Just jump on the comet!" they cheerfully cried.

I asked the wise planets, "What's my fate, oh please?"
Uranus just snorted, sending me to my knees.
"Your path is absurd, full of twists and pranks,
Just dance with the stars and give thanks to the janks!"

The cosmos, a canvas, with joy as my muse,
Oracles winked, said, "Forget all the blues."
With each playful riddle, I twirled with delight,
For who needs the answers when laughter takes flight?

So I cherish the journey, whatever the game,
With cosmic comedians, I'll never feel shame.
In the galaxies vast, I found freedom to roam,
In the heart of the chaos, I finally felt home!

Celestial Currents and Cosmic Waves

In the vacuum, a laugh does bloom,
Space dust tickles, it lights up the room.
Galaxies giggle, they spin and sway,
Who knew stars loved to dance all day?

Meteor showers, with sparkling flair,
Comets sneezing with cosmic air.
Black holes joking, a playful trap,
Don't fall in, you'll miss the next lap!

Alien beings on spaceships vast,
Play poker with planets, having a blast.
Gravity's a friend, but it's quite a tease,
Pulling your snacks with a gentle squeeze.

And when you spot Orion at night,
Give him a nod, he's quite a sight.
In the expanse where the fun's been spun,
The universe laughs; we're all part of the fun!

Astral Trek Beyond the Lights

Strap on your boots, the stars are bright,
Time to go trekking in the endless light.
Aliens asking for a selfie or two,
'Look at my spaceship! How about you?'

Asteroids wobble, a clumsy dance,
Whirling through space, not missing a chance.
'Catch me if you can!' they all shout loud,
Rockets zoom past, feeling so proud!

Nebulae giggle, wrapped in their haze,
As stardust sprinkles like confetti displays.
Planets play tag in a jovial race,
We cheer them on, feeling their grace!

So grab your snacks, let's make a toast,
To the galaxies swirling, we love the most.
With humor in hand, we'll sail through the skies,
In our starry adventures, laughter will rise!

Questing Through Cosmic Shadows

In shadows of planets where whispers roam,
We search for answers far from home.
Aliens giggle in dark, hidden bays,
While moons make popcorn, they're cooking away!

Fuzzy meteors with glittery tails,
UFOs spinning, they just can't fail.
Through fields of stars, we glide and slide,
Eclipses winking, what a cosmic ride!

Laughter echoes in craters and voids,
Playful like children, no need for theroids.
Jumping through shadows with a gleeful shout,
Searching for wonders, there's no doubt!

So as we quest through this darkened sprawl,
Let's giggle and munch on the cosmic ball.
For every riddle and shadow we find,
A chuckle awaits, oh, it's truly kind!

The Oath of Starlit Journeys

We pledge to roam amid stars so bright,
Every twinkle a promise, a pure delight.
Napping on comets, how absurdly sweet,
While space whales sing their celestial treat!

With star maps in hand, we plan our prance,
Through voids of laughter, we happily dance.
Galactic hitchhikers, we ride the light,
Making new friends, oh, what a sight!

Décor of moons and laughter so bold,
In the universe vast, we'll never grow old.
Stretched on a nebula, sipping on dreams,
Finding our way in the night's funny schemes!

So here's to the journeys, both silly and grand,
Where fun's an adventure, and we take a stand.
Starlit, we wander, with giggles in tow,
In this cosmic dance, let the good times flow!

Light Years to Understanding

In a spaceship made of dreams,
We race through fields of beams.
A snack break near a cosmic whale,
We laugh and sip on stardust ale.

Galaxies spin with a wink,
Stars giggle as we sink.
Caught in a black hole of thoughts,
We ponder all the things we sought.

Aliens join us for a dance,
Every twirl is quite the chance.
Who knew space could be so bright?
We stumble, trip, and lose our sight.

But in the end, we find our way,
As planets twirl in utmost play.
Understanding may take some time,
But laughter makes the journey rhyme.

Constellations of the Soul

Pointing out stars that look like cats,
Giggles echo where wisdom chats.
My soul's a donut, round and sweet,
With sprinkles of joy, can't be beat!

There's Orion sipping cocoa warm,
While Pleiades channeling a charm.
Each star a thought, each twinkle a grin,
Mapping my heart, where to begin?

A constellation of silly dreams,
Where nothing's quite as it seems.
The universe winks, then starts to hum,
"Let's make a plan and have some fun!"

In the night, we scribble glee,
Absurdity's key to just be me.
The journey's big, yet all is whole,
In the dance of my colorful soul.

The Universe Within

Inside my head is a swirling space,
Where thoughts collide in a silly race.
Stars explode with wild delight,
Launching dreams into the night.

Nebulas formed from late-night snacks,
Galaxies built from laughter tracks.
A black hole here swallows my chores,
While comets soar through snack-filled stores.

Asteroids made of fluffy socks,
Orbiting all the dorky blocks.
Every hiccup, a supernova,
A giggle fits, a cosmic do-over.

Exploring within is quite a blast,
In my chaotic space, I'm never last.
Through cosmic giggles and shining light,
I find my purpose, oh what a sight!

Chasing Comets of Intention

With a net made of hopes, we chase the stars,
Dodging asteroids, avoiding cars.
A comet streaks and swirls like fate,
We giggle at how we contemplate.

Burning bright with wishes like fireflies,
Plans in hand, and no goodbyes.
Each tail we chase, a laugh we find,
A journey filled, yet well-defined.

Meteor showers turn into pranks,
As we float along starry banks.
The universe snickers, "Can you dance?"
In cosmic rhythm, we take a chance.

With comets swirling all around,
We discover joy in every sound.
Intentions spark like shooting stars,
Chasing fun, we erase all scars.

In Search of Celestial Harmony

I sat on a star, chewing on light,
Watching the planets dance in the night.
They stumbled and twirled, oh what a sight,
I laughed so hard, I fell out of flight.

Galaxies giggled, what a loud cheer,
They whispered their secrets, so silly, so clear.
"Why find your purpose?" they echoed near,
"Just grab some stardust and sip cosmic beer!"

Asteroids rolled by, playing tag with my dream,
They wore little hats, how absurd it did seem.
With every weird turn, I burst out a scream,
"Is there a plan?"—was that just a meme?

In the end, I found, beneath twinkling sheen,
Perhaps it's all fun, just like a routine.
So I danced with the cosmos, a bright cranky queen,
Whirling 'round purpose, like I was a bean!

Comets of Consciousness

Comets raced by with a trail of wide grins,
They shouted, "Great journey! Come join in our spins!"
But I just tripped over some cosmic pin,
And rolled with the laughter, where chaos begins.

Black holes were laughing, or maybe they cried,
"Lose your way often, and take things in stride!"
With each swirling dive, there was nothing to hide,
Except for that awkward white dwarf's misguide.

Space-time was tickling the edges of fun,
As quasars were popping like balloons in the sun.
I asked, "Is it work, or is it all done?"
They said, "Just embrace the wild ways we run!"

So I cruised through dimensions, on sugar and glee,
Finding my rhythm, a galactic jamboree.
With laughter and pranks, I giggled with glee,
In a universe crazy, just let yourself be!

Orbits of Meaning

Planets keep spinning, who knows what's the goal?
Jupiter's giggling, swirling round like a troll.
Every orbit I take feels like a wild stroll,
Thoughts bouncing like meteors—what a strange roll!

The moons played cards, trapping light in their hands,
"Do we have purpose?" they exchanged our demands.
We tossed sanity out, just focused on bands,
Dancing on rings, while ignoring the stands.

I chimed in with chuckles, "Maybe it's fate,
To laugh at the voids and just contemplate.
Why seek for a meaning, like it's a debate?
Let's just crack jokes while we orbit, it's great!"

So I basked in the chaos, a mischievous bliss,
As galaxies winked at each humorous twist.
In the quest for my purpose, I found that sweet kiss,
Of laughter that brightened, every starry abyss!

Between Stars and Silence

Caught in hushed whispers, the stars had a chat,
"Is purpose a thing, or just a strange spat?"
They twinkled and giggled, while spinning like that,
And I eavesdropped closely, wearing my best hat.

In voids of confusion, where silence got loud,
Nebulae murmured beneath starlit shroud.
"I think we're just here to dance with the crowd,"
So I twirled with delight, feeling merry, not cowed.

Asteroids chuckled, they kept rolling by,
"Questions are good, but it's fun to just fly!
Why think about purpose when you've got the sky?"
So I dove into laughter, as moments went by.

Between stars and silence, I found a grand joke,
That life's just a hoot, a cosmic poke.
In the dance of existence, I happily stoke,
The flame of good humor—a bright binding cloak!

Echoes of the Celestial Path

In a universe vast and wide,
Aliens dance with comets as their guide.
One asked, 'What's our job in this show?'
The other replied, 'It's just to glow!'

Stars chuckle as they flicker bright,
While planets spin like tops at night.
A black hole said, 'I'm on a diet!'
But it swallows everything in sight!

Constellations gossip and tease
About a moon that's lost its keys.
'Where'd they go?' laughed a little star,
'By the sun, no doubt, it's gone too far!'

So here we are, on our grand tour,
Searching for more, but who knows for sure?
With telescopes aimed and minds ablaze,
Let's laugh at the cosmos and its quirky ways!

Navigating the Nebula of Meaning

In swirling mists of cosmic delight,
A spaceship captain shouts, 'Hold on tight!'
His crew is lost in a game of chess,
While asteroids bump and cause a mess.

They asked a quasar, bright and bold,
'What's the secret to life, if told?'
It winked and said, 'Try not to fret,
Just have some fun, and don't place a bet!'

A wormhole winked—yes, it was sly,
Said, 'Take the leap and aim for the sky!'
They flew right through without a care,
Came out the other end with a new pair!

So let's embrace chaos and the thrill,
On this starry ride, let's twist and spill.
With laughter ringing through empty space,
We'll dance through constellations, quicken our pace!

Threading Through the Tapestry of Time

In the fabric of time, a stitch went wrong,
A little time traveler sang a song.
'Where am I now?' she giggled with glee,
'Is this the age of dusty TV?'

Knitting moments, she tangled a bit,
Looped a dinosaur right into her skit.
'Oh dear!' she gasped, 'What a funny hat!'
The dino just roared, 'I'm cool, look at that!'

With memories woven of joy and strife,
We patch together the tapestry of life.
Laugh a little louder, and enjoy the climb,
For every thread is a glorious rhyme!

So here we are, with needle and thread,
Sewing up stories, letting laughter spread.
No matter the age or the cosmic design,
Let's knit up some fun, for it's all so fine!

Stardust Melodies of Existence

Floating on stardust, a cosmic parade,
Jupiter juggles while Venus gets laid.
Mars plays the trumpet, it's quite the scene,
As Saturn spins records—oh, what a dream!

Asteroids waltz in a glittering haze,
Dancing through space in a wild ballet.
A neutron star hums a quirky tune,
While galaxies giggle—and so does the moon!

On this trip through space, let's twirl the night,
As comets take center stage, oh what a sight!
With each little twinkle, a chuckle expands,
While black holes grumble—'Let us lend hands!'

So come join the fun, don't you be shy,
In the grand concert of life, you shouldn't pass by.
With laughter and melody filling the air,
Let's jive with the cosmos, let go of despair!

www.ingramcontent.com/pod-product-compliance
Lightning Source LLC
Chambersburg PA
CBHW071852160426
43209CB00003B/517